MW00815585

The Gift of Serving

The DAVE Volunteer Model™

Dr. Nancy Whitfield

The Gift of Serving: The DAVE Volunteer Model™

© 2014, Nancy Whitfield

Published by:
NanData Consulting, LLC
T/A The Leader's Lightship™
Chesapeake, VA
http://www.leaderslightship.com

All rights reserved. Any use of this material requires
prior written permission of the publisher.

ISBN: 978-0-9905464-1-2

Cover art by Dr. Nancy Whitfield
Author photograph by Lexie Hatcher
The DAVE Volunteer Model™, PAST-SEEK™,
and The Leader's Lightship™ are all trademarks of
NanData Consulting, LLC.

Scripture quotations taken from the New American
Standard Bible®
Copyright © 1960, 1962, 1963, 1968, 1971, 1972,
1973, 1975, 1977, 1995
By The Lockman Foundation
Used by permission. (www.Lockman.org)

Content from this book is also used in the seminar
The Gift of Serving: The DAVE Volunteer Model™
presented by Dr. Nancy Whitfield. Additional
information may be found at
http://www.leaderslightship.com.

Table of Contents

Preface

This book would not be possible without many people who have invested in me without abandon! I place great value on all the wonderful teachers and professors who have made such a difference in my life and encouraged me to be a lifelong learner.

I am blessed with an incredibly supportive circle of friends who sustain my spirit, light the spark of hope, and encourage me in using my gifts, including Joe Fournier, Dr. Lisa Fournier, Dawn Kennedy Levering, Rev. Bob Robinson, Brenda Sims, Charity Stephens, and the members of my One Voice Professional

Christian Writers Group. A huge thank you goes out to family members who have supported me through all of life's valleys and mountaintops, including my parents, L. W. and Jeanette; my grandparents, George, Elsie, Ellis, and Lillie; my sister, Susan and her family; my son, Michael; and my aunt and writing mentor, Dr. Elsie Craig, who continues to edit my work from heaven.

Gratitude also goes out to a number of people who supported my efforts by providing feedback, offering suggestions, or pointing me toward valuable resources, including Vicki Bradner, Susan W. Hatcher, Dawn Kennedy Levering, Roxanne Mills, Charity Stephens, and Jeanette Whitfield.

Both those who have allowed me to serve as well as those who have served alongside me have enriched my understanding of the role of volunteers. Thank you for these lessons in the learning laboratory of real life!

Finally and most importantly, for all things I give glory and thanks to God.

Prologue

As I was preparing to provide a presentation for a local community group, I explored a number of different ideas for the topic. A friend suggested that, based on her experience, many organizations just do not have a good handle on how to manage and maximize their volunteer workforces. Her comment hit home with me because I, too, had experienced a number of instances in which I had volunteered but things did not go as I thought they would.

Given that I had also led volunteer teams, I started to think about what strategies I learned to employ that fostered successful volunteer relationships. I thought about what types of volunteer arrangements had been fulfilling to me when I volunteered my time, energies, and talents in organizations. And, after all, I was going to be providing this presentation to – you guessed it – a volunteer organization!

As a professional educator, I have found that stories and memory tools (such as mnemonics) often help my students remember information. Applying these tools to the material in the presentation resulted in The DAVE Volunteer Model™ and ultimately this book. The story you will read about DAVE is based upon and adapted from one I wrote in my doctoral program while at Regent University as part of my final doctoral manuscript. Names and characters used in this and other stories and examples are fictional and do not represent actual people.

If you are a volunteer, if you lead groups of volunteers, or if your organization benefits from the work of volunteers, I hope this book will provide insight toward making those relationships successful and productive!

AS EACH ONE HAS
RECEIVED A SPECIAL GIFT,
EMPLOY IT
IN SERVING ONE
ANOTHER
AS GOOD STEWARDS
OF THE MANIFOLD
GRACE OF GOD.

- 1 PETER 4:10 (NASB)

Introduction

According to the Corporation for National and Community Service (www.volunteeringinamerica.gov), there were almost 7.9 billion hours of volunteer time offered by over 64 million Americans in 2012. While the argument can be made that the value of volunteer efforts far surpasses anything that can be measured in dollars and cents, this federal organization calculated the value of these volunteer efforts in monetary terms to be approximately $175 billion.

Opportunities for people to volunteer exist across all areas of the community, including corporate settings, non-profit settings, community groups, professional groups, religious organizations, schools, and governments to name a few. Those who fill the volunteer ranks likewise come from a cross-section of the community, drawing on individuals from all walks and stages of life, the military, and even programs in companies that support corporate social responsibility efforts in the community.

Some organizations depend heavily on volunteers to meet their mission and goals. No matter how pervasive the use of volunteers is in the organization, there is one point that cannot be ignored: without people, organizations cannot exist. People **are** the organization. When the availability of volunteers or volunteer hours declines, these organizations find themselves scrambling to fill needed slots. In my experience with leading volunteers, recruiting and training new volunteers requires a large investment, both in time and in other resources.

It is no wonder, then, that organizations that use volunteers frequently track and report a variety of volunteer statistics. These numbers appear as membership counts, hours of service provided, quantity of projects staffed, etc.

Quantifiable benchmarks are often reported to corporate home offices and can be found in newsletters, brochures, and on organizational web sites.

For instance, a volunteer organization comprised of members may be highly focused on membership numbers: how many new members joined; how many memberships lapsed; how many meetings members attended, etc. Understanding the metrics in an organization is clearly an important part of an effective

---

The volunteer organization typically exists to make a difference.
It has a *social purpose*.

---

management effort. If the leadership focuses solely on how to reach certain targets in the membership numbers, however, it risks missing the most important focus of all: whether the organization is achieving its desired outcomes.

The volunteer organization typically exists to make a difference. It has a social purpose. To this end, it becomes important to consider whether organizations are focusing on tracking the results in terms of the social purpose or whether they are merely counting how many volunteers they trained, the number of members they recruited, or the quantity of existing members they were able to retain on the roll.

As we begin this exploration, it is important to keep in mind that every situation is different and must be considered on its own merits. This book is meant to open a conversation on the topic of healthy volunteer relationships, but is by no means exhaustive in its approach. You, whether acting as part of an organization or whether offering your time and resources as a volunteer, must consider the best course of action and make your own decisions within the specifics of your situation.

This book discusses some key points for volunteer organizations to consider as they move beyond just tracking the numbers. It also is intended to provide an enlightened view to prospective volunteers when weighing their options about where to invest their time and talents. Toward these objectives, we begin with *The Story of DAVE*.

The Story of DAVE

Many organizations, such as churches and community groups, have outreach programs of various kinds. When someone is sick or there is a death in the family, for instance, members and volunteers may deliver meals. When a new neighbor moves in, a welcoming committee may send a basket or make a visit. When an organization identifies a prospective client who might benefit from the goods or services the organization provides, such as someone who is newly diagnosed with a disease or needs support services offered by the organization, someone may be designated to make contact with them.

Consistent with this approach, a number of churches commission a ministry in which volunteers take bread to the homes of those who recently visited the church, an activity usually considered an outreach of hospitality and evangelism. In this role, the church likely wants a volunteer to deliver the bread who has good interpersonal skills, is knowledgeable of the church and what it offers, and is welcoming and friendly. It needs someone who engages the visitor, finds out more about them, and invites them to return in the future. It likely wants the person to exude a warm, caring demeanor that is non-threatening and easy-going. In other words, this position calls for someone who is a people person, who can connect with others, and has the ability to create relationships easily. Consider the following story about a bread ministry volunteer named DAVE.

The Story of DAVE

The hospitality committee chair at the church is running short on volunteers to deliver bread this week, so she asks DAVE if he will help out. DAVE has never worked in this ministry area before, but he says he will be happy to help. DAVE picks up the bread along with a little slip of paper with the address on it and heads out to make his delivery.

Already familiar with the neighborhood, he veers quickly into the driveway of the recent church visitor's home. He leaves the car running, hurriedly jumps out, and sprints up to the visitor's front door, taking the steps two at a time. He rings the doorbell. Ring! No one answers. He hastily rings it again, pushing the button just a little bit harder as if that will summon someone more quickly. *RING!*

The door finally opens. A small-framed elderly woman greets him with a smile and begins to say a quiet, "Hello..."

Before she can finish this first word of greeting, DAVE says dutifully and cheerily, "Here! I'm from the church! I'm supposed to give you THIS!"

DAVE shoves the loaf of bread into the surprised little lady's hands and, without further ado, abruptly turns, jumps off the stoop onto the lawn, and dashes back to his running car. He slams the door and speeds off down the quiet shady tree-lined street, slightly squealing his tires as he goes.

The stunned little lady tells her neighbor, who happens to know someone at the church, about this curious encounter. The story makes *its way, as stories often do, back to the hospitality chair at the church. She is mortified.*

"Oh, didn't you know?" another bread ministry volunteer responds to the hospitality chair. "DAVE's a take-out delivery driver in the evenings."

DAVE's job requires that he get from point A to point B in the shortest time possible, and there is no time for small talk. Actually, DAVE is considered one of the most efficient delivery drivers at his store.

The next Sunday, the hospitality chair seeks DAVE out and finds him talking with some other churchgoers. She launches into a lecture right in the middle of the hallway, expressing her distinct displeasure and ridiculing him for having failed to carry out the assigned tasks.

DAVE's eyes widen. Dumbfounded and caught off guard by this public scolding, he apologizes and quickly departs in embarrassment. Not only does DAVE not offer to help in the bread ministry again, no one has seen him at church since.

The DAVE Volunteer Model™

None of us would want to find ourselves in DAVE's shoes. Unfortunately, there are volunteers in real-life situations whose experiences are like DAVE's. These experiences cause them to reconsider whether they will continue offering their valuable time, talent, and energies even though they have a strong desire to serve. How can organizations be better equipped to support their volunteer workforces?

The DAVE Volunteer Model™ is an easy mnemonic to remember, designed to help both those who recruit and train volunteers as well as those who serve as volunteers. The model encompasses four key areas: *description, alignment, values,* and *environment.* The hope is that this approach provides a straightforward framework within which volunteers and volunteer organizations effectively consider their opportunities toward successful and rewarding partnerships.

DESCRIPTION

ALIGNMENT

VALUES

ENVIRONMENT

The following sections explore each area of the model.

DESCRIPTION

One of the common challenges I encountered as a volunteer over the years was the lack of clear expectations about what I was supposed to do. How many times have you heard side conversations in organizations about how so-and-so was assigned to complete a task, and yet somebody else had to jump in to help? Or maybe the person did not do the task properly, and it had to be redone by someone else? Or, worse yet, it was not done at all or was done poorly? These types of situations may reflect negatively on the organization and adversely affect future projects, public perception, or the desire of other volunteers to participate.

We will discuss three areas regarding how the details of a volunteer job are communicated: the job description itself, levels of authority, and full disclosure.

DESCRIPTION
A
V
E

First, having a job description for each volunteer role could help to avoid the outcomes noted above. In your organization, do you have volunteer job descriptions? If someone is to head up a fundraising dinner, for instance, has someone clearly articulated the expectations to the person who agrees to lead this function? Does the assigned volunteer even know what has to be done to make the fundraising dinner happen? Too often leaders of volunteers may think that the expectations are self-evident when, in reality, they are not.

Think of your own volunteer situations.

- How often have you received an actual job description detailing the responsibilities and expectations of the volunteer role you accepted?

- How many times have you agreed to serve as a volunteer only to find that you have more questions about what to do and how to do it than you have answers?

If the volunteer role is to serve as an organizational officer, there may be something regarding job responsibilities written in the bylaws. There could be a listing of duties or expectations that either the organization has developed formally or that one volunteer passes to the next as succession occurs. As has more often been the case in my own experience, there may be nothing in writing.

Not all volunteer roles require a long formal written description. A short paragraph or two may suffice depending on the circumstances.

SCENARIO 1

Volunteers who are selling lemonade on Saturday for the baseball team are less likely to have a written job description. The need to understand the expectations of what they are to do, however, is still just as important.

❑ How is the money to be handled?
❑ Who counts the money?
❑ What is the ratio of lemonade mix to the water?
❑ Where do they get ice refills?
❑ Whom do they call when they run out of cups?
❑ How much do they charge for the large cup vs. the small cup?
❑ Are there food handling safety rules that need to be followed?
❑ What time is the stand to close?

While the form of the job description may fall anywhere between a formal written document, a more informally crafted checklist, or even a set of verbal instructions, of higher importance is assuring that the job description is both complete and communicated effectively and timely to the volunteer.

Second, besides carrying out the actual duties of the role itself, volunteers may face the need to make decisions in the course of their activities. It is important that they know the boundaries in such situations.

- What level of authority do they have?
- Are they at liberty to make purchasing decisions?
- Are they empowered to give something away for free, to offer a discount, or are they expected to account for every penny?

Unclear expectations about levels of authority and what a volunteer is permitted or not permitted to do can create difficult scenarios for both the organization and the volunteer.

SCENARIO 2

A community group is holding a carnival for children with special medical needs. The purpose is to provide a day of fun during which the children are the center of attention. Anne volunteers to work in a booth selling T-shirts and hats. The coordinator shows Anne how to scan the merchandise and ring up the sales on the cash register. The coordinator also posts a sign at the booth that says, "All sales final."

A young boy purchases a yellow T-shirt for his sister and returns a few minutes later. His sister is crying because she wants a blue one instead. The two T-shirts are the same price, so the volunteer makes the exchange and decides that she will pay for the returned T-shirt herself if necessary. After all, the whole purpose of the day is to make the children happy!

In the above scenario, the coordinator posted a sign but did not discuss its meaning or provide any direction to Anne about returns or exchanges. As a result, Anne applied her best judgment by considering the organization's values and the purpose of the event in making a decision.

Finally, sometimes organizations are so desperate for people to help that they downplay the reality of what is expected or needed. The failure to establish and communicate expectations in an open and honest way can also affect the goodwill of volunteers. Consider this scenario about an eager new member of the organization.

SCENARIO 3

Joe, a veteran member of the organization, is tasked with finding a new chairperson for the annual fundraising event. Everyone he has asked has declined due to the significant time commitment required. He approaches a new member, Hank, who feels honored to be asked, about taking on this role.

Joe stretches the truth by explaining that most of the planning has already been done, thereby significantly reducing the time commitment required. At the first meeting, Hank discovers that several key tasks remain outstanding and a much greater investment of time will be required than he anticipated based on the earlier discussions.

This approach of minimizing expectations may result in a short-term positive result of getting someone to agree to take on the position or fill the need; however, the longer-term results are arguably *highly ineffective*.

A number of potential undesirable outcomes could ensue.

- Trust is eroded between volunteers and the organization.

- Volunteers become disillusioned because the organization expects them to give of themselves toward the organization's mission, but cannot reciprocate with truthful expectations.

- Volunteers feel that they were set up to fail instead of supported to succeed.

- The volunteer steps away unexpectedly, leaving the organization with an unanticipated void to fill. There is often a significant investment of resources to recruit, train, and bring on new volunteers. Doing this repeatedly for the same position may consume precious limited resources that could have been used for other purposes.

- Even worse, public relations are affected, possibly influencing whether future potential volunteers wish to dedicate their efforts or resources to the organization, or even whether donors wish to continue to financially support the organization.

This situation is like eating sour candy. The coating on the outside is sweet and yummy, but once that coating melts away, what is left is a sour taste that lasts much longer than the sweet.

The organization should be forthright with an accurate depiction of what the volunteer role requires in terms of time, energy, skills, and aptitudes.

To summarize, clear and complete job descriptions, whether written or oral, are important in helping volunteers know what the organization expects of them. Establishing well-defined levels of authority helps volunteers understand boundaries and meet expectations.

When the organization is forthright with an accurate depiction of what the volunteer role requires in terms of time, energy, skills, and aptitudes, there is less room for disillusionment. Overall, efforts in these areas set the stage for a more productive working relationship between the volunteer and the organization.

In support of this outcome, the PAST-SEEK™ method, an easy approach to building a job description, is described in the Appendix.

Suggested Action Items:

✔ Create a job description for volunteer roles.
✔ Communicate the job description accurately and fully.
✔ Establish and share relevant limits of authority.

ALIGNMENT

Now that we have established that volunteers need to know what to do, it is important to recognize that they also need to feel that they can be successful at what they do. This outcome is supported when there is alignment between the individuals' aptitudes, skills, and experience and the roles we are asking them to fulfill.

D
ALIGNMENT
V
E

Take, for example, the manner in which many clubs and professional organizations approach volunteer leadership roles. It is not uncommon for individuals who serve in an officer position in an organization to find themselves engaged in a multi-year commitment during which they progress from roles like treasurer or secretary up to a vice president role and then to the presidency of the organization. While there are merits to this type of progression, such as allowing individuals to become familiar with different areas of the organization and how they operate, there are also potential drawbacks.

First, it may be harder to find someone who is willing to make such a multi-year commitment than to find someone who will do a particular job for a year. Second, as the individual moves up through the various officer positions, the skills needed in order to be successful in each role change. Consider the following situations.

- The treasurer's role involves the need for an attention to detail with handling financial information and the ability to track and monitor funds. For the individual who finds balancing his own personal checkbook a challenge, this type of volunteer role may not be a good fit.

- The secretary position typically writes the correspondence, keeps the meeting minutes, and communicates with the organization's members. For someone who does not like to write or who does not use technology for activities such as emailing or word processing, this role may not be the best fit.

- If the vice president position plans the organization's programs and events, the person in this role probably needs good organizational skills, aptitude in detailed preparation, and the ability to recruit others to help. For the person who prefers to do things spontaneously, this may not be the most effective assignment. Meeting space and speakers for programs likely need to be scheduled and planned well in advance.

- The president's position typically requires someone who can conduct meetings and is comfortable speaking in front of groups. For the individual who suffers from a fear of public speaking or who does not like to be in the limelight, this type of position may create more stress than enjoyment for them.

Questions to ask include:

- Why does the organization require that people move through this progression of offices if they have exceptional skills in one area and want to continue to serve?

- What if they only want to serve for a year or two in an area they enjoy and do well and not rotate through each of the officer positions?

The treadmill response of, "This is how we've always done it," is the usual answer. If a volunteer wants to expand her skills in a certain area and take on a role that will help her do that, that is fantastic. There are alternatives that the organization can employ such as mentoring and matching volunteers with others who can teach them new skills. Outside of this situation, it is important to find out what this person does well in order to more effectively assign tasks.

The volunteer organization has a great opportunity to engage people in roles that maximize their strengths to the benefit of the mission. In my experience, people generally do not want to take on jobs that are outside their capabilities. While most people know what they do well, on a few occasions, I have encountered people who think that they are more proficient than they really are at something. After a friend recently reminded me of this potential, I began to consider why this might happen. It is possible that they have not used certain skills in a while and are a little rusty, or maybe they have honestly overestimated their abilities or misunderstood the job requirements. Regardless of the reason, part of the leader's role is to make decisions about how best to use volunteers based on the skills they actually have, or are willing to develop.

In addition, just because volunteers have a particular skill does not mean that they wish to use it in a volunteer setting. For example, those who cook all day long in their job may not want to be in the kitchen preparing food for a dinner meeting, even though they are very skilled in this area. Roofers who spend all day in the hot sun may not want to spend their Saturday fixing the roof at the organization's clubhouse.

Think of your own volunteering experiences. When you offered to volunteer, did anyone ask you what you wanted to do, or were you just ushered into a role because it was empty and needed filling? Interestingly, people might actually say what they enjoy doing and what they do well if someone would only ask them!

Sometimes the most dedicated and reliable volunteers perform poorly because organizational leaders allow them, or worse yet, expect them, to take on a role for which they are not well suited. In countless situations, I have seen a devoted volunteer's sense of duty outweigh his best judgment about whether he can actually do the job. The volunteer takes on the job out of a sense of obligation and a true desire to help, understanding that the organization has a specific need that it is having difficulty fulfilling. The volunteer is not, however, energized by this particular opportunity or well-equipped to carry out the required duties.

Leaders should help volunteers feel great about what they do by putting them in places where they SHINE!

The assertion can be made that organizations not only have an opportunity to place people in the right positions, but also a responsibility to do so. The importance of proper placement may be especially high if a poor fit results in a volunteer experiencing embarrassment, undue attention, or scrutiny.

Leaders should help volunteers feel great about what they do by putting them in places where they shine!   The scenario below is a personal example of how those who care about me value my strengths.

SCENARIO 4

I joke with my family and friends that I am "culinarily challenged." In fact, I have a wooden plaque in my kitchen that reads:

"I only have a kitchen because it came with the house."

Luckily, there are others in my family who have great gifts in the culinary area. Instead of cooking, I contribute to family gatherings in ways that draw upon my strengths. I often help to set up or clean up. Because I am a musician, I may even provide music for the occasion!

In summary, organizations can do themselves and their volunteers a big favor by asking volunteers what they do well and what kinds of activities they enjoy doing.   Leaders should carefully consider the situation of a volunteer who takes on a role solely out of a sense of obligation. Volunteer leaders who look for ways to incorporate the strengths of volunteers into the needs of the organization have taken a step not only toward meeting organizational goals, but also toward building powerful intrinsic rewards for volunteers when they experience true joy in serving.

Suggested Action Items:

- Find out what people do well.
- Match the skills and aptitudes of the volunteer to the needs of the organization.
- Let the best skills of volunteers shine!

VALUES

Values are a vital element when considering volunteer relationships. To put it simply, values are the things that are of importance to us. They drive how we make decisions and evaluate what is right and what is not. Our values form throughout our lives, often influenced by our upbringing, our relationships, and our belief systems. Both individuals and organizations operate on a set of values.

D
A
V ALUES
E

Organizations typically have some sort of statement that identifies its values. Values are often:

- articulated through mission statements or codes of conduct;

- communicated by the types of decisions that are made; and,

- conveyed by the conduct that is accepted and promoted within the organization.

Some of the biggest clashes I have witnessed in volunteer settings are those in which the values of the organization and those of the volunteer are different. While not all conflict can be avoided, there are steps organizations may take to help support harmony in the volunteer relationship when it comes to values.

First, if the organization is not clear about its values internally, it is likely not able to articulate them effectively to others. By clarifying and documenting its core underlying values, the organization takes a conscious step toward establishing two important elements: what is truly important; and on what basis it intends to function and make decisions. As noted earlier, there are a number of ways in which organizations can identify and memorialize their values, including writing a values statement, incorporating expectations within the mission objectives, or by establishing a code of conduct.

Second, values differ among organizations and individuals. Organizational and individual values often include more universal types of expectations such as honesty, integrity, respect, politeness, etc. There may also be values, however, that are specific to the organization based on its purpose. Examples include a religious organization that has a code of personal conduct that it expects volunteers to abide by, or an animal welfare organization that values the lives of animals to the point of prohibiting euthanasia.

The values systems in place are as varied as the organizations themselves. When engaging new volunteers, one area to consider is an exploration of values alignment. When the values systems are too far apart, there is a higher likelihood of missing the mission intent and, consequently, for more conflict. I have known people who, without asking, naively believed that others had values similar to their own.

While most organizations generally accept and expect core values such as honesty and integrity, sometimes it might be the deeper and more specific values unique to the individual organization that warrant exploration and discussion.

SCENARIO 5

The coordinator from a community research organization asked a prospective volunteer to review its statement of values and expectations. Afterwards, the coordinator asked for the volunteer's thoughts on the values statement, which led to a candid dialogue. Although he was interested before the conversation, the volunteer became even more committed once he realized that the organization's values and his values were so similar.

In my experience, the approach noted in Scenario 5 is not a prevalent practice. This suggests to me that there may be opportunities for organizations and volunteers alike to engage in more of this type of dialogue.

The exploration of values is a two-sided effort: the organization considers whether its values align with the potential volunteer's, and the volunteer evaluates whether her values are consistent with the organization's values. In Scenario 3 from the last chapter regarding finding a fundraising chairperson, clearly Hank valued honesty and full disclosure. The organization may have held these same values; however, Joe may not have been exhibiting them in his own behavior.

If we are asking people to do something that is inconsistent with their own values, the probability of a successful outcome is *significantly reduced.*

There is one particular point to keep in mind when thinking about values. If we are asking people to do something that is inconsistent with their own values, the probability of a successful outcome is *significantly reduced*.

When there is a clear understanding of values and values are well-aligned, this condition sets the stage for a more harmonious working relationship.

Suggested Action Items:

✍ Define your organization's values.

✍ Learn about the values of volunteers.

✍ Look for consistency between them.

✍ Look for areas in which values are different.

✍ Evaluate the results.

ENVIRONMENT

The volunteers who come into our organizations usually do so because they want to. Granted, there may be instances in which volunteers are assigned in order to pay back a debt to society; however, the vast majority of the volunteer situations I have encountered exist because the individual asks, or agrees after being asked, to share his time, talents, resources, and energies on behalf of the organization.

Given that volunteers are offering their time and gifts, usually for little compensation other than satisfying an intrinsic desire toward a cause or mission in which they believe, volunteer organizations have to recognize the precariousness of this relationship and the importance of the organizational environment.

D
A
V
Environment

In short, people already have enough stress in their lives. They have family obligations, work obligations, and community obligations. When faced with the choice of whether to continue to engage in a volunteer role in an environment that creates a lot of stress, people will likely disengage from the area for which they have the least to lose. When reviewing this list of obligations, there is a much greater potential for negative consequences by walking away from a job, a family, or other similar commitments. There is typically much less to lose by walking away from a volunteer assignment. Volunteers may quickly revoke their willingness to commit precious resources when the environment is not a healthy or happy one. Consider the following scenario.

SCENARIO 6

This young woman is excited to be serving on a newly formed task force to help advance a cause that is close to her heart. She arrives with energy and optimism to her first committee meeting.

As the meeting progresses, she is surprised to learn that the task force members are strongly divided in opinion on several critical issues, resulting in a heated discussion, which continues via email even after the meeting adjourns.

The volunteer quickly arrives at the unfortunate conclusion that the role in which she thought she would be happily engaged toward addressing this important cause has turned into a source of personal stress instead of joy.

This scenario drives home the importance of building awareness about the type of environment that organizations cultivate for volunteers who offer their time and talents.

- Do the volunteers enjoy being there?
- Do they look forward to their assigned duties?
- Do they bring excitement and joy to the task?
- If they had a choice, which in fact they typically do, is this the place they would choose to spend their time, especially given the competing priorities in their lives?

In addition to the question of whether people find the organizational environment one in which they wish to engage, there is also the question of whether they feel their contributions are noticed. Valuing and appreciating volunteers goes much further than giving them a pin or a certificate for their efforts. This activity encompasses the whole of the volunteering experience.

- Are volunteers' ideas important?
- Does anyone listen when volunteers have a problem, or are individuals left to figure it out on their own?
- Does anyone say "thank you?"
- Is there any recognition of the sacrifices volunteers make in choosing your organization as the place where they spend and invest their energies?

Even when budgets are tight, the simplest gestures can sometimes mean the most when thanking volunteers.

Even when budgets are tight, the simplest gestures can sometimes mean the most when thanking volunteers. A warm greeting, a heart-felt personal note, or even a muffin and a cup of coffee can make volunteers feel respected and valued. The key is in expressing appreciation in genuine and personal ways. Shaking someone's hand and telling them how their efforts make a difference is vastly different than receiving a form letter and a certificate in the mailbox six months later.

Besides specific acts of appreciation, organizations can use other ways to convey how much they value their volunteers. For instance, creating an environment in which people interact with respect and harmony can be a welcome respite. Investments in teambuilding and matching people with others who have complementary skills can be an enriching experience. Maintaining healthy communication and feedback are also components to supporting healthy volunteer relationships.

Organizations that want to attract and keep good volunteers should create an environment where *people want to be!*

Organizations that want to attract and keep good volunteers should create an environment where *people want to be!*

By creating a place where ideas are welcome, people feel accepted, and individuals who show up really want to make a difference, they create an environment where people **want** to spend their time.

Suggested Action Items:

🖎 Create a place where people want to spend their time.

🖎 Remember to say "thank you" in genuine and personal ways.

🖎 Focus on maintaining a healthy environment.

Revisiting
The Story of DAVE

Now that we have discussed the four areas — *description, alignment, values,* and *environment* — we will revisit *The Story of DAVE.*

DESCRIPTION
ALIGNMENT
VALUES
ENVIRONMENT

Let's reread the story one more time with a fresh perspective given the concepts and ideas discussed in this book.

The Story of DAVE

The hospitality committee chair at the church is running short on volunteers to deliver bread this week, so she asks DAVE if he will help out. DAVE has never worked in this ministry area before, but he says he will be happy to help. DAVE picks up the bread along with a little slip of paper with the address on it and heads out to make his delivery.

Already familiar with the neighborhood, he veers quickly into the driveway of the recent church visitor's home. He leaves the car running, hurriedly jumps out, and sprints up to the visitor's front door, taking the steps two at a time. He rings the doorbell.

Ring! No one answers. He hastily rings it again, pushing the button just a little bit harder as if that will summon someone more quickly. RING!

The door finally opens. A small-framed elderly woman greets him with a smile and begins to say a quiet, "Hello..."

Before she can finish this first word of greeting, DAVE says dutifully and cheerily, "Here! I'm from the church! I'm supposed to give you THIS!"

DAVE shoves the loaf of bread into the surprised little lady's hands and, without further ado, abruptly turns, jumps off the stoop onto the lawn, and dashes back to his running car. He slams the door and speeds off down the quiet shady tree-lined street, slightly squealing his tires as he goes.

The stunned little lady tells her neighbor, who happens to know someone at the church, about this curious encounter.   The story makes its way, as stories often do, back to the hospitality chair at the church. She is mortified.

"Oh, didn't you know?" another bread ministry volunteer responds to the hospitality chair. "DAVE's a take-out delivery driver in the evenings."

DAVE's job requires that he get from point A to point B in the shortest time possible, and there is no time for small talk. Actually, DAVE is considered one of the most efficient delivery drivers at his store.

The next Sunday, the hospitality chair seeks DAVE out and finds him talking with some other churchgoers. She launches into a lecture right in the middle of the hallway, expressing her distinct displeasure and ridiculing him for having failed to carry out the assigned tasks.

DAVE's eyes widen. Dumbfounded and caught off guard by this public scolding, he apologizes and quickly departs in embarrassment. Not only does DAVE not offer to help in the bread ministry again, no one has seen him at church since.

Consider your own thoughts as you attempt to answer each of the following questions.

DESCRIPTION

Did DAVE understand the goals and purpose of the bread ministry?

Did DAVE understand how his role related to the mission of the ministry?

Did DAVE have a clear description of his job duties?

Was there effective communication about what he was to do and how?

ALIGNMENT

Were the needs of the volunteer position well aligned with DAVE's skills and gifts?

Was there an exploration of alignment between DAVE's gifts and the needs of the bread ministry?

VALUES

Were DAVE's values consistent with those of the hospitality ministry?

Did DAVE have a clear understanding of the values?

Did the hospitality ministry area have a clear understanding of DAVE's values?

Were there assumptions made about values? If yes, what where they?

ENVIRONMENT

Was the volunteer organization's environment a healthy one?

Did DAVE feel appreciated for having jumped in to help at the last minute?

Why has DAVE not come back to the church?

Could DAVE's leaving the church altogether have been avoided?

SUMMARY

What kind of lasting impacts might this interaction have had on:

- DAVE?
- The little lady?
- The bread ministry?
- Other bread ministry volunteers?
- The church?

If you were going to rewrite the story of DAVE to be a successful one, how would you write it?

In summary, the hospitality chair apparently did not describe to DAVE the expectations related to delivering the bread. DAVE did not know that he was supposed to become acquainted with the person to whom he was delivering the bread. He did not know that spending time with the recipient was one of the most important elements of the task. Likewise, the hospitality chair may have assumed that DAVE knew the mission and goals of the bread ministry when in fact he did not really understand them.

DAVE's skills appear strong in the areas of efficiency and delivery. He may even have had great interpersonal skills that were required for the job; however, he may not have exercised them because he did not <u>know</u> that the job required them. The value in making the delivery quickly seems at odds with the value of building relationships, thereby creating a situation in which the objectives of the bread ministry were compromised.

Was it DAVE's fault that he did not meet the expectations? One could assert that the hospitality chair did not give proper information and direction to DAVE. One could also assert that DAVE jumped into his volunteer role eagerly without asking for clarification or direction. Either way, the result ended up being the same: the desired outcomes were not met, the hospitality chair lost an energetic and dedicated volunteer, and the church may have lost an attendee. If DAVE were involved in other volunteer activities at the church, his departure would also affect these areas. Was the situation one in which DAVE had the opportunity to really shine?

As illustrated here, a bad experience can snowball into all kinds of unexpected impacts that affect, in a variety of unfortunate ways, the organization, the volunteer, and even those intended to benefit from the volunteer service. On the other hand, think of all the wonderful and synergistic outcomes that are possible with just a few strategic changes!

The Volunteering Checklist

Both organizations and volunteers benefit when there is a good fit and when expectations are clear. The approach to achieving this outcome is different depending on whether you are representing the volunteer organization or whether you are the potential volunteer.

FOR THE ORGANIZATION

If you are part of an organization that uses volunteers to meet its mission and objectives, consider the following list of questions. Where appropriate, check off which suggested action items you have already done and note those that are relevant to your situation that still need attention.

	Questions	Suggested Action Items
☐	**1. Do we have a job description for this volunteer role?**	Write a job description. It can be as simple as a paragraph or as formal as a full-blown written explanation. (See the Appendix for the PAST-SEEK™ approach.)
☐	**2. Have we communicated clearly and effectively the expectations and requirements of this volunteer role?**	Set up a time to review the job description with the volunteer.

	Questions	Suggested Action Items
☐	**3. Did we confirm that the volunteer understands the expectations?**	Ask the volunteer to describe his understanding of the expectations to verify a shared understanding.
☐	**4. Have we identified and communicated the limits of authority for this volunteer role?**	Specify limits of authority in the job description and explain them to the volunteer.
☐	**5. Do we know what volunteers do well?**	Identify strengths and aptitudes of potential volunteers.
☐	**6. Is there a good fit between the job description and the strengths and skills of the volunteer?**	Evaluate the fit between the job description and the strengths and skills of the volunteer.

	Questions	Suggested Action Items
☐	**7. Is the use of this volunteer in this role going to allow both the organization and the volunteer to shine?**	Set aside time to evaluate the organizational fit of this volunteer.
☐	**8. Is this an area in which the volunteer wants to serve?**	Ask the volunteer both what he wants and likes to do.
☐	**9. Have we identified our organizational values?**	Write down organizational values and share them with the volunteer.
☐	**10. Have we explored the volunteer's values?**	Ask the volunteer about his own values and what is important to him.

	Questions	Suggested Action Items
☐	**11. In what ways do the organization's values and the volunteer's values align and in what ways do they differ?**	Compare the values of the organization and those expressed by the volunteer.
☐	**12. Are our values and the volunteer's values sufficiently aligned to be a good fit?**	Evaluate the fit between the volunteer's values and the organization's values.
☐	**13. Do we create a place where volunteers want to come to share their time, experience, and skills?**	Ask volunteers about their experiences working with our organization.

Questions	Suggested Action Items
☐ **14. Do we make an effort to thank people for their contributions on a regular basis? Do we know what volunteers value in terms of appreciation?**	Ask what types of appreciation volunteers find meaningful. Schedule expressions of gratitude as part of the organization's ongoing operational activities.
☐ **15. How may volunteers provide feedback, ask questions, or communicate concerns?**	Clearly communicate to volunteers what channels are available to them for providing feedback, asking questions, or communicating concerns. Provide phone numbers, web sites, written resources, etc.

FOR THE VOLUNTEER

If you are a volunteer who is thinking about investing your time and energies with an organization, consider the following list of questions and suggested action items in preparing to serve. Check off the ones that you have already addressed and note the ones that are pertinent to your situation that warrant attention.

	Questions	Suggested Action Items
☐	**1. Have I reviewed a job description for this volunteer role?**	Ask for a written job description. For some positions, this may be a formal document. For others, it may only be a paragraph or two describing the role. See the Appendix for a sample approach to creating one.
☐	**2. Do I understand clearly the expectations and requirements of this volunteer role?**	Meet with the supervisor or volunteer coordinator to review expectations and ask any questions you may have.

Questions	Suggested Action Items
☐ **3. Did someone explain the expectations to me or am I relying primarily on my own understanding?**	Follow up to assure that expectations have been clearly communicated. Be careful not to assume too much; ask for clarification.
☐ **4. Do I understand the limits of my authority in this volunteer role?**	Discuss the limits of authority with the volunteer coordinator and identify whom to ask if you need additional approval.
☐ **5. Which of my skills and abilities will I use in this role?**	Review the job description to verify which types of skills are needed.

	Questions	Suggested Action Items
☐	**6. Are my skills and abilities aligned well with the job description for this role?**	Review the job description to see if your skills and those needed for this job are well aligned.
☐	**7. Am I confident that I can contribute in a meaningful way and that my contributions will draw on my strengths?**	Discuss your strengths with the volunteer coordinator and evaluate whether this job is a good fit based on those strengths.
☐	**8. Is this an area in which I really want to serve, or am I just stepping into this role out of a sense of obligation?**	Consciously evaluate your motive for serving. Realize that serving in a role for which you do not feel well suited may not be ideal.

Questions	Suggested Action Items
☐ **9. Do I understand the organization's values, and has the organization communicated them to me?**	Ask the volunteer coordinator for the values statement of the organization. Read and discuss them with the volunteer coordinator to assure you have an accurate understanding.
☐ **10. Have I had the chance to share my values with the organization?**	Share your values related to this volunteer role with the volunteer organization.
☐ **11. In what ways do my values align with the organization's values and in what ways do they differ?**	Evaluate whether your values and those of the organization are consistent with each other.

Questions	Suggested Action Items
☐ **12. Are my values and the organization's values sufficiently aligned to be a good fit?**	Based on the values evaluation, determine whether there is a good fit between your values and the organization's values.
☐ **13. Is this organization a healthy environment in which I enjoy spending time and want to serve?**	Think about how you feel when you volunteer. Consider whether this activity brings joy and fulfillment.
☐ **14. Is it important for me to be recognized for my contributions and, if so, how?**	Communicate with the volunteer coordinator any expectations for recognition or for anonymity if desired.

Questions	Suggested Action Items
☐ **15. What channels are available to me for providing feedback, asking questions, or communicating concerns?**	Clarify the methods, processes, and structures for communicating feedback, questions, or concerns.

Summary

The DAVE Volunteer Model™ provides a structure for remembering four key areas related to this discussion about developing and nurturing volunteer relationships.

DESCRIPTION
ALIGNMENT
VALUES
ENVIRONMENT

Many of us have given the gift of serving, and many organizations have benefited from this gift.

My hope is that organizations may be poised to create healthier volunteer interactions and foster the growth of valuable volunteer contributions by investing a little time in reviewing and considering these four basic areas. I hope that organizations continue to recognize the great value of the gift and that they appreciate even more those who give it.

This hope also extends to individual volunteers in terms of being better equipped to evaluate potential volunteer opportunities, including looking for strong alignment with values, skills, and abilities. My wish is that individuals who make this valuable gift of serving do so by drawing on and sharing their strengths in gratifying ways, and that they encounter great joy in serving.

Appendix

The PAST-SEEK™ Job Description

An easy approach to building a job description is to use a format called PAST-SEEK™.

1. Fold a piece of paper into quarters (in half and in half again).
2. Unfold the paper.
3. Label each of the quadrants on one side of the paper as follows (PAST):
    o Purpose
    o Authority
    o Structure
    o Tasks

4. Turn the paper over.

5. On the opposite side, label the remaining
    four quadrants as follows (SEEK):

    o Skills

    o Experience

    o Education

    o Knowledge

Fill in the details for each quadrant of the
page. Below are some example questions to help
get you started with filling in each quadrant.
These questions are not exhaustive. Through
using the tool, your organization will probably
find additional, organization-specific questions
that are appropriate to include in the various
sections. If you are a volunteer, you may find this
format helpful when discussing and clarifying the
expectations of a volunteer role with the
organization.

PAST-SEEK™ Job Description

SIDE 1 - PAST

Purpose	Authority
Structure	Tasks

PAST-SEEK™ Job Description

SIDE 2 - SEEK

Skills	Experience
Education	Knowledge

The PAST Section

PURPOSE

- Why is this job needed?
- How does this job support the mission and objectives of the organization?
- In general, what does this job do?
- How long of a commitment does this job require (e.g., a year, multiple years, one afternoon, a week, etc.)?

AUTHORITY

- What level of authority does this position have?
- What decisions can this person make without supervision?
- What decisions require a higher level of approval?
- How does the approval process work?
- Who would the person go to for decisions requiring additional approval?

STRUCTURE

- What is the work schedule for this job (e.g., days, times, number of hours, etc.)?
- What is the relationship of this job to other jobs in the organization?
- What kinds of interactions, including internal and external, are required to be successful in this job?
- How does this job fit into the organizational structure?
- How will the person receive feedback about performance?
- Who supervises this volunteer role?
- To whom does the person go for assistance or problem solving?

TASKS

- What exactly are the tasks the person in this job is to perform?
- What standards must the person meet in performing the job?
- In what order should the person complete the tasks?

- What are the checklists, directions, bylaws, or procedures available regarding these tasks?
- What equipment or supplies are needed to complete the job?
- Where would the individual find these and other pertinent resources?

The SEEK Section

SKILLS

- What types of skills must the person be proficient in to complete the job?
- What types of equipment must the person be able to use?
- What languages must the person speak?
- What types of interpersonal skills are expected?

EXPERIENCE

- What kind of background or experience is required for this job?
- Must the person have done this type of job before and if so, for how long?

EDUCATION

- What special certifications or licenses are required for this position (e.g., food handling, electrical trade license, etc.)?

- What types of training or education must this person have to complete this job?

- What training or orientation should the organization provide to this volunteer about this role (e.g., safety orientation, equipment use, confidentiality, etc.)?

- When and where will the training be provided?

KNOWLEDGE

- What does the person need to know to be successful or qualified for this job?

- What knowledge resources are available to the person performing this job?

About the Author

Dr. Nancy Whitfield is President of The Leader's Lightship™. She earned a Doctor of Strategic Leadership (DSL) from Regent University and a Master of Science in Management with a concentration in leadership and organizational effectiveness from Troy University. Her career spans more than three decades in a variety of organizational settings and has involved leading a number of large mission-critical change initiatives.

Dr. Whitfield is especially interested in the areas of leadership and organizational effectiveness. A writer and featured speaker in local, regional, and national venues, she enjoys teaching graduate and undergraduate courses in business and leadership. Beyond her academic pursuits, Dr. Whitfield is also an accomplished musician, songwriter, and worship leader.

Further information is available on the web.

www.leaderslightship.com

www.giftofserving.com

Notes

Notes

42478491R00059

Made in the USA
Charleston, SC
30 May 2015